Meringue Girls x

First published in the United States of America
in 2014 by Chronicle Books LLC.

First published in the United Kingdom
in 2013 by Square Peg.

Library of Congress Cataloging-in-Publication Data available.

ISBN 978-1-4521-3353-9

Manufactured in China

Designed by Well Made Studio.
Photographs by David Loftus.
Styling by Jo Harris.
Illustrated titles and paint washes by Kenn Goodall.

Ferrero Rocher is a registered trademark of Ferrero SpA.
Cadbury's Crunchie is a registered trademark of Cadbury Limited.

10 9 8 7 6 5 4 3 2

Chronicle Books LLC
680 Second Street
San Francisco, California 94107
www.chroniclebooks.com

Meringue Girls x

CHRONICLE BOOKS
SAN FRANCISCO

This book has interactive content

Download the free Layar App

Find and scan pages with the Layar logo

Discover video content

THIS BOOK IS DEDICATED TO
EVERYONE WHO DREAMS
ABOUT LEAVING THEIR 9 TO 5.

JUST GO FOR IT.

introduction

Introduction

Cupcakes, cake pops, and macarons have had their day. Now is the time for meringue.

Meringue Girls are making meringues cool again! We handcraft the best meringues you have ever tasted: mallowy in the middle, with a melt-in-the-mouth texture.

In this book, we aim to demystify meringues, which are notoriously hard to make. We will show you the easy way to ensure foolproof meringues every time.

We'll share our fresh, modern, and colorful take on classic meringue recipes, giving them a Meringue Girls twist with exciting flavor combinations.

Our book includes heaps of gift ideas, fun ways to get the kids involved, easy and impressive summer dessert ideas, and indulgent winter dinner party finales.

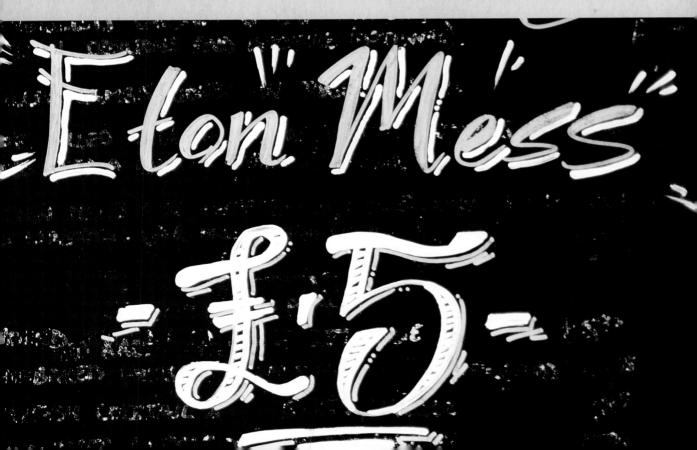

OUR MERINGUES ARE NATURALLY GLUTEN FREE.

WE ARE BIG ON FLAVOR. THE POSSIBILITIES ARE ENDLESS— JUST USE YOUR WILLY WONKA CREATIVE FLAIR.

WE RECOMMEND USING THE BEST-QUALITY NATURAL INGREDIENTS,

SUCH AS FREE-RANGE EGGS, ORGANIC SUGAR, AND ARTISANAL DARK CHOCOLATE AND COCOA.

ABOUT THE MERINGUE GIRLS

Alex Hoffler

Alex is London born and bred. Following university and two years working at a major London marketing agency, she traveled for a year, taking cooking courses in India, Thailand, Cambodia, and Vietnam.

She then completed a year's course at Leiths School of Food and Wine, where she received a first-class diploma. She currently does food styling for various publications.

Stacey O'Gorman

Growing up in Auckland, New Zealand, Stacey had a passion for food from a young age. She trained at Auckland University of Technology, achieving a diploma in culinary arts.

To widen her experience, Stacey spent a year abroad to explore the culinary world, honing her skills in kitchens along the way. In one such kitchen, she met Alex, with whom she shared an epicurean passion, and a partnership was born.

The Girls

Alex and Stacey formed the Meringue Girls after working together in a restaurant in Hackney. They bonded over a love of sweet things, especially meringues. From big launches and pop-ups to weddings and gift boxes, they have worked with amazing clients, including **Whistles, Jimmy Choo, L'Oréal, H&M, *Vogue, Elle,*** and ***Marie Claire.***

TIPS AND TECHNIQUES

Meringues are all about volume!

Here are some points to remember to ensure maximum voluminosity.

🍫 The recipes in this book use U.S.-size large eggs. (At Meringue Girls, we use free-range liquid egg whites—which work really well—so that we don't have hundreds of yolks swimming in our fridge like once upon a time.)

🍫 Make sure your egg whites are free of yolk and shell—crack and separate them carefully and check the whites before you start to whisk. The best way to get rid of a speck of yolk is to use a bit of shell to fish it out.

🍫 For best results, we recommend weighing eggs and solids. A measuring cup is fine for liquid ingredients such as cream, water, and juice. A digital kitchen scale is an essential tool for every serious meringue maker.

🍫 Cream of tartar stabilizes your whites and makes a stiffer but less glossy mixture; if your whites are not super fresh, add about ⅛ tsp per white before whisking.

🍫 We use superfine sugar for most meringue methods as the fine grain dissolves very quickly. We heat the sugar in the oven so that it dissolves even more quickly, resulting in a smooth and glossy mixture. If the sugar hasn't been allowed to dissolve and the mixture is grainy when it goes into the oven, the meringues will often leak sugar syrup during baking.

🍫 A stand mixer is your best friend (we use a KitchenAid mixer), but it is also possible to make meringues with an electric handheld whisk. Hand whisking is fine for making small batches (3 egg whites max for us), but for larger amounts, you'll need big biceps and a lot of willpower.

Use clean equipment. Greasy bowls and utensils will deflate the lovely volume you have created. We often wipe out our mixing bowl with lemon juice to make double sure it's spotless. Grease tends to cling to plastic bowls and spatulas, so use metal or glass ones.

The biggest mistake with meringue making is adding the sugar before the whites are totally stiff. If you add the sugar too early, your meringues will never acquire the stiff consistency you want.

Volume is made by stretching the elasticity of the egg whites to their full capacity. The whites are stiff enough when you can hold the bowl upside down without them dropping out.

Vinegar lends a chewiness to meringues. Add ½ tsp to your stiff whites for a really mallowy middle.

Baked meringues can be covered in plastic wrap or placed in an airtight container and stored in a cool, dry place for up to 2 weeks. Do not refrigerate.

MERINGUE GIRLS MIXTURE

Our meringue to sugar ratio is very easy to remember: it is one part egg whites to two parts sugar. A large egg white weighs 30 g, so use 60 g of superfine sugar per egg white. *But always weigh your whites, as eggs vary in size.*

½ BATCH

150 g superfine sugar
   (¾ cup)
75 g egg whites
   (from about 2½ eggs)

1 BATCH

300 g superfine sugar
   (1½ cups)
150 g egg whites
   (from about 5 eggs)

DOUBLE BATCH

600 g superfine sugar
   (3 cups)
300 g egg whites
   (from about 10 eggs)

Preheat the oven to 400°F.

Line a rimmed baking sheet with parchment paper, pour in the sugar, and put the baking sheet in the oven for about 5 minutes, until the edges of the sugar are just beginning to melt. Heating the sugar will help it dissolve in the egg whites more quickly and help create a glossy, stable mixture.

Meanwhile, make sure the bowl and whisk attachment of your stand mixer are free from grease. Pour the egg whites into the bowl. Whisk on low speed at first, allowing small bubbles to form, then increase the speed to high and continue whisking until the egg whites form stiff peaks and the bowl can be tipped upside down without the whites falling out. Stop whisking just before the whites take on a cotton-woolly appearance; if they do, they have been over-whisked, and the egg protein has lost some of its elasticity.

By now, the sugar should be ready to take out of the oven.

With the whites stiff and while whisking again at high speed, add one big tablespoonful of hot sugar after another to the bowl ensuring that the whites come back up to stiff peaks after each addition. Don't worry about small clumps of sugar, but avoid adding large chunks of caramelized sugar from the edges of the baking sheet.

Once you have added the sugar, continue to whisk on high speed for 5 to 7 minutes. Rub a bit of the mixture between your fingers, and if you can still feel gritty sugar, keep whisking at high speed until the sugar has dissolved, the mixture is smooth, and the bowl is a bit cooler to the touch. The meringue will continue to thicken up during this stage. You know it is ready to use when it forms a nice smooth, shiny peak on the tip of your upturned finger.

To find out how to flavor, stripe, pipe, and bake your meringue kisses, turn to pages 30 to 35.

FLAVORING

Traditionally, meringues are simply flavored with chocolate, vanilla, or nuts. But you don't have to stick with just those. We've come up with some winning flavors to try, but feel free to experiment and create your own—Willy Wonka style!

When it comes to using flavored kisses in desserts, you can pick and choose to suit your taste. Sometimes we've suggested the flavor if there is a clear winner.

Meringue mixture is temperamental, so you need to work quickly. Be careful not to add too much flavoring, especially oily nuts or liquid, as it will deflate the mixture.

For all the flavors that follow, use one batch of Meringue Girls Mixture (page 26).

CHOCOLATE:

Use **3 tbsp good-quality cocoa powder, sifted**. Fold 1 tbsp into your meringue mixture until just combined. Spoon the mixture into your piping bag, cut the tip (if necessary), and start piping. Once you have piped out all of your chocolate kisses, dust the tops with the remaining 2 tbsp cocoa.

HAZELNUT:

Use **3 tbsp finely ground hazelnuts**. Fold 1 tbsp into your meringue mixture and paint the inside of your piping bag with stripes of **natural amber food coloring**, then spoon the mixture into your piping bag, cut the tip (if necessary), and start piping. Once you have piped out all of your hazelnut kisses, sprinkle with the remaining 2 tbsp ground hazelnuts.

LAVENDER:

Fold **½ tsp natural lavender extract** into your meringue mixture. Paint the inside of your piping bag with stripes of **natural purple and blue food colorings**, then spoon the mixture into your piping bag, cut the tip (if necessary), and start piping.

COCONUT:

Use **½ cup/50 g unsweetened dried coconut**. Fold ¼ cup/25 g into your meringue mixture until just combined. Spoon the mixture into your piping bag, cut the tip (if necessary) and start piping. Once you have piped out all of your coconut kisses, sprinkle the peaks with the remaining ¼ cup/25 g coconut.

PASSION FRUIT:

Use **3 tsp freeze-dried passion fruit powder**. Fold into your meringue mixture, then paint the inside of your piping bag with stripes of **natural yellow and purple food coloring**. Spoon the mixture into your piping bag, cut the tip (if necessary), and start piping.

CINNAMON:

Use **1 tbsp ground cinnamon**. Fold ½ tbsp into your meringue mixture until just combined. Spoon the mixture into your piping bag, cut the tip (if necessary), and start piping. Once you have piped out all of your cinnamon kisses, dust the tops with the remaining ½ tbsp cinnamon using a sieve.

HOT CROSS BUN:

Fold **1 tsp pumpkin pie spice, 1 tsp ground cinnamon, and 1 tbsp finely chopped candied orange or lemon peel** into your meringue mixture until just combined. Paint the inside of your piping bag with stripes of **natural brown food coloring**, then spoon the mixture into your piping bag, cut the tip (if necessary), and start piping.

PISTACHIO AND ROSE WATER:

Use **8 tbsp/50 g finely ground pistachios**. Fold 2½ tbsp into your meringue mixture along with **1 tsp rose water**. Paint the inside of your piping bag with stripes of **natural red food coloring**, then spoon the mixture into your piping bag, cut the tip (if necessary), and start piping. Once you have piped out all of your kisses, sprinkle with the remaining 5½ tbsp ground pistachios.

GREEN TEA:

Fold **1 tbsp matcha green tea powder** into your meringue mixture. Paint the inside of your piping bag with stripes of **natural green food coloring**, then spoon the mixture into your piping bag, cut the tip (if necessary), and start piping.

STRAWBERRY AND BLACK PEPPER:

Use **3 tbsp freeze-dried strawberries ground into a fine powder and ½ tsp ground black pepper.** Fold into your meringue mixture and paint the inside of your piping bag with stripes of **natural red food coloring**, then spoon the mixture into your piping bag, cut the tip (if necessary), and start piping. Once you have piped out all of your kisses, crack a tiny bit of black pepper over each meringue.

GINGER:

Fold **2 tbsp ground ginger** into your meringue mixture. Paint the inside of your piping bag with stripes of **natural orange food coloring**, then spoon the mixture into your piping bag, cut the tip (if necessary), and start piping. Top with thin strips of fresh or crystallized ginger, if you fancy.

MANUKA HONEY:

Fold **3 tbsp dried manuka honey powder** into your meringue mixture until just combined. Paint the inside of your piping bag with stripes of **natural amber food coloring**, then spoon the mixture into your piping bag, cut the tip (if necessary), and start piping.

RASPBERRY:

Use **3 tbsp freeze-dried raspberries ground into a fine powder**. Fold this into your meringue mixture and paint the inside of your piping bag with stripes of **natural pink food coloring**. Spoon the mixture into your piping bag, cut the tip (if necessary), and start piping.

VANILLA BEAN:

Split lengthwise and scrape out the **seeds from 1 vanilla bean** and fold into your meringue mixture until just combined, making sure the seeds are evenly dispersed. Spoon the mixture into your piping bag, cut the tip (if necessary), and start piping.

CHAI:

Use **1 tbsp chai powder and 1 tsp cardamom seeds** (from about 2 pods), finely crushed. Fold the chai powder and ½ tsp of the cardamom seeds into your meringue mixture until just combined. Paint the inside of your piping bag with stripes of **natural amber food coloring**, then spoon the mixture into your piping bag, cut the tip (if necessary), and start piping. Once you have piped out all of your chai kisses, sprinkle with the remaining ½ tsp crushed cardamom seeds.

STRIPING AND PIPING KISSES

Striping

Meringue kisses are a fun way to shape and color meringues. You can use them in a variety of different desserts, including cake tiers and petits fours. All our meringue kisses are hand-piped and bite-size, and each has its own unique organic shape and color.

To make striped kisses, whip up a batch of Meringue Girls Mixture (page 26) and turn a large disposable piping bag or a reusable one with a ⅞-inch diameter opening inside out. Invert the bag over a jug or bottle so that it holds itself up. Using natural food coloring and a clean paintbrush, paint wide stripes from the tip of your piping bag to halfway down (about five stripes). Roll the bag so the painted side is the inside, folding the edges over to make a sturdy vessel.

Carefully spoon your meringue mixture into the piping bag, rolling the sides up. You need to pack the meringue mixture in tightly, ensuring there are no air bubbles. Pinch the top of the bag closed, gently pushing the mixture in.

If using a disposable piping bag, with sharp scissors, cut the tip of the bag so that the opening measures ⅞ inch in diameter.

To get the meringue mixture flowing, twist the top of the piping bag to push the meringue to the bottom. Pipe small dollops onto the four corners of your baking sheets (if you are using a full batch of Meringue Girls Mixture, you will need a couple of baking sheets). Line the baking sheets with parchment paper; the meringue dollops will act as glue and stick the paper to the sheets.

You are ready to start piping!

Piping

Hold the piping bag vertically with both hands, securing the twisted top with your dominant hand and placing your other hand halfway down the bag. Use the top hand to apply pressure and the lower hand to control the flow of the meringue. Squeeze the bag to form a kiss with a 2-inch base, and then lift up the bag while releasing some pressure so that the meringue forms a big peak at the top. Space the kisses about ¾ inch apart. Piping perfect kisses takes practice, so don't worry if you don't get it right the first time. One batch of Meringue Girls Mixture will make about 35 kisses.

To bake your kisses, position racks in the upper and lower third of the oven and preheat your oven to 200°F. Slide the baking sheets into the oven and bake for 30 to 40 minutes until the kisses are easily lifted off the parchment paper, with their bases intact. Let cool completely on the baking sheets. Stored in an airtight container in a cool, dry place, the kisses will keep for up to 2 weeks.

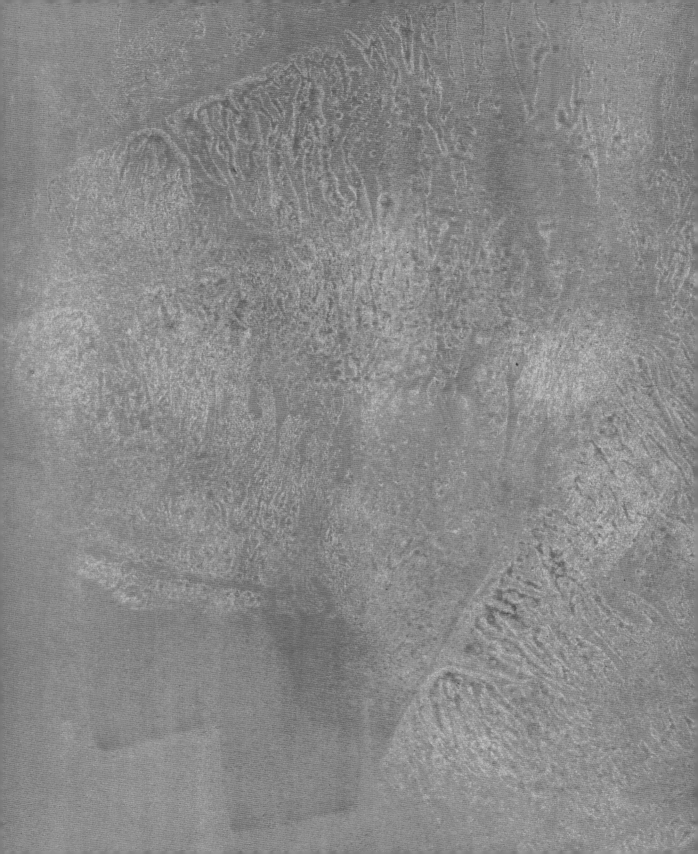

KISS

Recipes

FILLINGS FOR KISSES

Sandwich your meringue kisses around a variety of tasty fillings and pop them on the table after dinner for the sweetest petits fours. Mix and match kiss and filling flavors to create great taste sensations.

CHOCOLATE GANACHE:

Melt **1¾ oz 70% dark chocolate, chopped,** in a heatproof bowl set over a saucepan of simmering water (don't let the bowl touch the water) or in a microwave-safe bowl in the microwave on high for 1 to 2 minutes. Pour in **3½ tbsp heavy cream**. Mix quickly with a spoon. The ganache should have a thick, silky consistency.

PEANUT BUTTER:

Mix **3 tbsp crunchy peanut butter** with **2 tsp confectioners' sugar.** The filling should have a thick consistency and just the right balance of salty and sweet.

LEMON AND POPPY SEED:

Mix **3½ tbsp of Lemon Curd with Lemongrass** (page 140, or good-quality store-bought lemon curd) with **½ tsp poppy seeds and 2 tbsp cream cheese** at room temperature. This should have a thick, silky consistency and be a great balance of sour and sweet.

COFFEE CREAM:

Whip **3½ tbsp heavy cream** to stiff peaks. Add **a small espresso shot** (about 2 tbsp) to the cream along with **1 tbsp confectioners' sugar** and whisk until the cream has a thick, smooth, and silky consistency.

NUTELLA BUTTERCREAM:

Whisk **3½ tbsp unsalted butter** (room temperature) with **¼ cup/75 g Nutella** until smooth, then whisk in **¼ cup/ 25 g confec- tioners' sugar** and **a pinch of sea salt** until light and fluffy.

RAINBOW WEDDING TIER

This meringue wedding tier is a great alternative if you are bored with the standard wedding cake and dessert cupcake tier, and want your wedding to stand out from the rest. You can take our recommendations for meringue kiss flavors or just choose colors and flavors to suit your mood. Remember that you will need more meringues for the larger bottom layers than the smaller top layers. Make your kisses in batches and store for up to 2 weeks in an air-tight container until you are ready to assemble your masterpiece.

FILLS A LARGE 7-LAYERED TIER

12 separate batches Meringue Girls Mixture (page 26), flavored according to the suggestions at right or to suit your taste

FOR THE FULL RAINBOW EFFECT, WE RECOMMEND THE FOLLOWING FLAVORS AND NUMBERS OF BATCHES:

CHOCOLATE (SEE PAGE 30), 3 BATCHES

RASPBERRY (SEE PAGE 32), 2 BATCHES

PISTACHIO AND ROSE WATER (SEE PAGE 31), 2 BATCHES

GINGER (SEE PAGE 32), 2 BATCHES

PASSION FRUIT (SEE PAGE 31), 1 BATCH (YELLOW STRIPES ONLY)

GREEN TEA (SEE PAGE 32), 1 BATCH

COCONUT (SEE PAGE 31), 1 BATCH

Make your meringue kisses following the instructions on pages 34 to 35.

On a 7-layer stand, build your wedding tier, starting from the bottom. On our tier in the photo, we have used approximately 90 chocolate kisses, 70 raspberry, 52 pistachio and rose water, 37 ginger, 25 passion fruit, 18 green tea, and 8 coconut.

KISS CANAPÉS WITH POMEGRANATE PROSECCO

Sometimes the simple things in life are best. Here we've paired up meringue kisses with our favorite bubbly. Heaven. This is perfect for a celebratory toast or for sharing with friends on a summer day.

SERVES 8

1 batch Meringue Girls Mixture (page 26), flavored with raspberry (see page 32), pistachio and rose water (see page 31), or strawberry and black pepper (see page 32)
¼ cup plus 2 tbsp heavy cream
1 tbsp confectioners' sugar
8 fresh raspberries

FOR THE POMEGRANATE PROSECCO:

1 cup pomegranate juice
One 750-ml bottle of prosecco, chilled
A handful of pomegranate seeds

For the canapés, make your meringue kisses following the instructions on pages 34 to 35.

In a medium bowl, whip the cream and sugar to stiff peaks, taking care not to overwhisk.

Assemble your canapés by placing eight of the prettiest meringue kisses on a beautiful serving platter. Dollop each kiss with 1 tsp of whipped cream and top with a single fresh raspberry.

To make the pomegranate prosecco: Pour 2 tbsp of the pomegranate juice into each of eight champagne flutes and top off with prosecco. Drop a few pomegranate seeds into each flute and serve with the canapés. Cheers!

MAYAN HOT CHOCOLATE WITH FLOATING KISSES

The Mayan flavors give this spicy hot chocolate a serious kick of winter warmth. Add a shot of smoky mezcal or tequila to turn up the heat. The meringue kisses ooze and goo like marshmallows once they hit the hot chocolate.

SERVES 4

½ batch Meringue Girls Mixture (page 26)
Cocoa powder, for dusting

FOR THE HOT CHOCOLATE:

1 fresh red chile
3 cups whole milk
5 cardamom pods, crushed
5 cloves
2 cinnamon sticks
2 star anise
¼ cup/50 g packed dark brown sugar, plus more as needed
1 tbsp good-quality cocoa powder
5¼ oz 70% dark chocolate, chopped
A splash of mezcal or tequila (optional)

Make your meringue kisses following the instructions on page 34 to 35. Dust four kisses with cocoa powder and set aside; reserve the rest for another use.

To make the hot chocolate: Slice the red chile lengthwise down the middle, retaining the seeds and all. Pour the milk into a medium saucepan. Add the sliced chile, the cardamom pods, cloves, cinnamon sticks, and star anise. Then add the brown sugar and cocoa powder. Place over low heat and slowly bring to a gentle simmer.

Once the spiced milk is simmering, strain it through a sieve into another saucepan to get rid of the spices and the chile. Place the milk back over low heat and add the dark chocolate. Stir until the chocolate has melted, then remove from the heat. Taste the hot chocolate and add more sugar if it needs it.

Pour your hot chocolate into mugs and add a splash of mezcal or tequila (if using) to each. Top with your beautiful cocoa-dusted meringue kisses and serve.

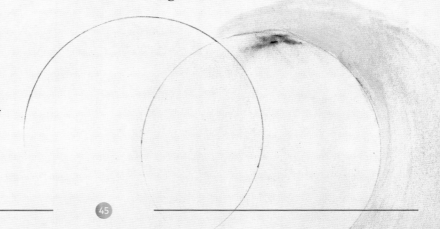

CHOCOLATE AND BEET BARBIE CAKE

This is the perfect cake for a little—or big—kid's party.

SERVES 12

1 batch Meringue Girls Mixture (page 26)

FOR THE CAKE:

1⅔ cups vegetable oil, plus more for greasing

2¾ cups/350 g all-purpose flour

2¼ cups/450 g superfine sugar

1½ cups/150 g good-quality dark cocoa powder

4 tsp baking powder

1 lb cooked and peeled beets

6 eggs

FOR THE ICING:

1¼ cup plus 3 tbsp heavy cream

1¾ cups/400 g cream cheese

¼ cup/25 g confectioners' sugar

1 Barbie doll (clothes and legs removed)

Barbie accessories

Divide the meringue mixture into six portions. Following the instructions on pages 34 to 35, form each portion into mini striped kisses in the color of your choice; use a piping bag with a ¾-inch opening to pipe kisses with 1-inch bases. (It's fine to pipe more than one color onto a single baking sheet.) These mini kisses will bake more quickly than regular kisses; bake them for about 20 minutes, or until they can be lifted off the parchment paper with their bases intact. Let cool completely on the baking sheets.

To make the cake: Turn up the oven temperature to 350°F. Grease an 8-inch springform pan and line the bottom with parchment paper. Grease an 8-inch ovenproof bowl (about 10 inches deep) and line it with parchment paper.

Sift the flour, superfine sugar, cocoa powder, and baking powder into a large bowl. Cut the beets into large chunks and add to a blender along with the eggs and oil. Purée until smooth. Pour the beet mixture into the dry ingredients and fold until combined.

Pour one-half of the batter into the prepared springform pan and the remaining batter into the prepared bowl. Bake the cakes for 40 minutes, or until a cake tester inserted into the centers comes out clean. Let cool for 15 minutes, then invert the cakes out of the pan and bowl and onto a wire rack. Peel off the parchment and let cool completely.

To make the icing: In a large bowl, whip the cream to stiff peaks, then add the cream cheese and confectioners' sugar. Continue to whisk until the mixture is smooth and stiff.

Bling out your Barbie however you'd like—goth or glam, it's up to you.

Set the flat cake layer (the one baked in the springform pan) on a cake platter. Spread with about 1 cup of icing in an even layer. Set the bowl-shaped cake on top, tapered-end up. Using a knife, trim the stacked cake to form a nice hoop-skirt shape.

With a long, slender knife (such as a bread knife), cut a 2-inch-deep hole in the center of the cake and insert Barbie to just below her waist. Spread the remaining icing over the cake, taking care to work around Barbie.

Carefully place meringue kisses on the cake, arranging one color at a time in a row around Barbie, starting at her waist and working down. Press the kisses lightly into the icing so that they stick and form a beautiful, colorful meringue-kiss skirt.

MERINGUE PROFITEROLES

Meringue kisses filled with whipped cream are by far the most delicious way to use up leftover meringue kisses. This works best when the kisses have dried out for a few days after baking as they will have a harder shell.

MAKES 35 KISSES

1 batch Meringue Girls Mixture (page 26), flavored to suit your taste and formed into 35 kisses (see pages 30 to 35), then dried out for up to 2 weeks

FOR THE COULIS (OPTIONAL):
¼ cup/30 g frozen raspberries
½ tsp honey
1 tsp water

FOR THE FILLING:
¾ cup heavy cream
1 tsp confectioners' sugar
¼ cup/30 g raspberry coulis or 1½ tbsp Lemon Curd with Lemongrass (page 140), to flavor the cream (optional)

Use a small, sharp knife to make a small hole in the base of each meringue kiss—just big enough for a very small piping tip to fit in it.

To make the coulis (if using): Pour the raspberries, honey, and water into a saucepan and bring to a boil. Turn down the heat and simmer gently for a further 5 minutes. Purée in a food processor until smooth and set aside to cool.

To make the filling: In a large bowl, whip the cream and sugar just until the mixture holds its shape (it tends to stiffen further in the piping bag). If you want, fold in the coulis or lemon curd.

Fit a piping bag with a small, round, plain pastry tip and spoon the cream into the bag. Pipe cream into each kiss through the hole, aiming to fill the center with as much cream as possible.

Eat quickly.

FERRERO ROCHER MERINGUE TOWER

A quirky play on the iconic Ferrero Rocher celebration tower—and a sign of good taste!

SERVES 8

1 batch Meringue Girls Mixture (page 26), flavored with hazelnut (see page 30)

FOR THE WHIPPED CREAM:
1 cup heavy cream
1 tbsp confectioners' sugar

FOR THE GANACHE:
7 oz 70% dark chocolate, chopped
¾ cup plus 2 tbsp heavy cream

Ferrero Rocher candies
Toasted and skinned hazelnuts
Edible gold leaf

Make your meringue kisses following the instructions on pages 34 to 35.

To make the whipped cream: In a large bowl, whip the cream and sugar just until stiff, taking care not to over-whisk. Set aside.

To make the ganache: Melt the chocolate in a heatproof bowl set over a saucepan of simmering water or heat it in a microwave-safe bowl in the microwave for 1 to 2 minutes on high, taking care not to let the chocolate burn. Once the chocolate has melted, fold in the cream just until combined. The ganache should be thick and silky.

Get out a flat serving platter, ideally one that's gold in color. Form the tower base by arranging meringue kisses in a triangle, with five kisses on each side forming the perimeter; glue the bases of the kisses to the platter with ganache. Build up the tower by stacking kisses on top, creating a pyramid that tapers to a single kiss, and using ganache and whipped cream as your cement. Fill in the gaps with Ferrero Rocher candies and hazelnuts, cementing them in place. Finish with small pieces of edible gold leaf.

summery

desserts

LOVE HEARTS WITH RHUBARB AND GINGER

A seriously cute and delicious dessert, this is ideal for Valentine's Day or a special occasion.

SERVES 6 TO 8

1 batch Meringue Girls
  Mixture (page 26)

FOR THE TOPPING:

2 or 3 rhubarb stalks
1 tbsp superfine sugar
¼ cup/35 g candied ginger

1 cup heavy cream
1½ tbsp confectioners' sugar

Position racks in the upper and lower third of the oven and preheat your oven to 200°F. Line two baking sheets with parchment paper. Fill your piping bag with the meringue mixture and, using meringue blobs like glue, stick the parchment to the baking sheets.

Pipe the outline of a heart, about 3 inches long and 5 inches wide on the parchment, then fill in the center with meringue. Build up the sides by piping two more layers on top of the original outline. Pipe five to seven more hearts in the same way on the baking sheets, spacing them at least ¾ inch apart. For a smoother, more organic look, dampen a finger and run it lightly over the base and edges.

Bake the hearts for 45 minutes, or until they can be lifted off the parchment with their bases intact. If the bases are still soft, return the hearts to the oven, turn off the oven, and leave to dry for 15 minutes. Let cool completely on the baking sheets.

To make the topping: Preheat the oven to 350°F. Cut the rhubarb stalks in half lengthwise if they are very thick, then cut crosswise into 2-inch pieces. Put them in a baking dish, sprinkle with the superfine sugar, and bake for 6 to 8 minutes, or until the pieces are softened but still hold their shape. Let cool. Cut the candied ginger into slivers.

In a medium bowl, whip the cream and confectioners' sugar to soft peaks.

Spread the whipped cream onto the hearts and top with the rhubarb and candied ginger. Serve right away.

STRAWBERRY-MERINGUE ICE LOLLIES

A fabulous treat to pull out of the freezer on a hot summer's day. These ice lollies will put a smile on everyone's face.

MAKES 6 LOLLIES

½ batch Meringue Girls
  Mixture (page 26)
¼ cup/50 g superfine sugar
¼ cup water
2 cups/250 g strawberries,
  hulled and cut in half
Juice of 1 orange

Make the Meringue Kisses following the instructions on page 34 to 35. Crumble six kisses into bits; reserve the rest for another use.

Bring the sugar and water to a boil in a medium heavy-bottomed saucepan over medium-high heat and boil for 5 minutes until syrupy. Leave to cool.

In a food processor, purée the strawberries until smooth. Stir the purée and the orange juice into the cooled sugar syrup.

Fill each of six ice-pop molds about one-quarter full of strawberry purée, then drop in a few bits of meringue. Pour in more purée and add more meringue until the molds are filled. (If you have any strawberry purée left over, freeze it in an ice cube tray and use the frozen cubes to chill fruity drinks.) Insert a stick into each mold and freeze the ice lollies until solid, at least 4 hours.

Unmold and serve right away.

RASPBERRY RIPPLE AND MERINGUE GELATO

Here's a great way of using up leftover baked meringues that have lost their middle gooeyness, or those that didn't turn out as pretty as you had hoped. This no-fuss ice cream doesn't require churning, so you can make it even if you don't own an ice cream machine.

MAKES ABOUT 1 QUART

2 cups/350 g raspberries
3 eggs
½ cup/100 g superfine sugar
1¼ cups heavy cream
1 batch Meringue Girls
   Mixture (page 26), formed
   into kisses (see pages 34 to 35)
   and broken into bits
Melted dark chocolate,
   for drizzling (optional)

In a small bowl, mash about two-thirds of the raspberries with a fork until smooth. Set aside.

In a medium heatproof bowl, whisk the eggs and sugar. Set the bowl over a saucepan of simmering water and beat with a handheld mixer until the mixture is thick and doubled in volume; this will take about 10 minutes. Remove the bowl from the saucepan and continue beating until the mixture has cooled to room temperature.

In a large bowl, use the handheld mixer to whip the cream to soft peaks. Using a rubber spatula, fold the whipped cream into the egg mixture, then gently fold in the meringue bits.

Pour about half of the gelato base into a 1-quart container, then spoon about half of the raspberry purée over the top. Pour in the remaining base, spoon the remaining raspberry purée over, and use a butter knife to swirl the purée into the base. Cover with plastic wrap and freeze for at least 5 hours, or ideally overnight.

Let the gelato stand at room temperature for a few minutes to soften slightly. Scoop into bowls or dishes and drizzle with melted chocolate, if you fancy a further flourish. Garnish with the remaining raspberries to serve.

LEMON MERINGUE CAKE

This cake has a little secret: it's filled with delicious lemon curd that oozes out when a slice is cut. It is an extremely tangy and moist cake. We use our Marshmallow Meringue (page 148) as a wonderfully gooey frosting.

SERVES 8

1 cup/225 g butter, plus
  more for greasing
1 cup plus 2 tbsp/225 g
  superfine sugar
4 eggs
2 tsp vanilla extract
1¼ cups/150 g self-rising flour
¾ cup/75 g ground almonds
Grated zest and juice of 2 lemons
A little milk, if needed
1 cup/400 g Lemon Curd
  with Lemongrass (page 140)
  or good-quality store-bought
  lemon curd
Marshmallow Meringue
  (page 148)

Preheat the oven to 350°F. Grease a 9-by-5-inch loaf pan and line it with a strip of parchment paper cut to fit into the bottom and up the long sides of the pan, with some overhang.

In your stand mixer fitted with the flat beater attachment, beat the butter and sugar on medium-high speed until light and fluffy, about 5 minutes. Beat in the eggs one at a time, then add the vanilla. Using a rubber spatula, fold in the flour, ground almonds, and lemon zest and juice. The batter should be soft enough to drop from a spoon; if it is too stiff, fold in just enough milk to get the proper consistency. Scrape the batter into the prepared loaf pan and smooth it out with the spatula.

Bake for 20 to 25 minutes, or until golden brown on top and a skewer inserted into the middle comes out clean.

Let the cake cool in the pan for 5 minutes, then invert it onto a wire cooling rack. Peel off the parchment, turn the cake right-side up, and let cool completely.

Use a melon baller or grapefruit spoon to scoop out a trough in the center. (The trimmings aren't needed for finishing the cake.) Fill the trough with the lemon curd.

Spread the Marshmallow Meringue over the surface. Brown the meringue with a kitchen torch or preheat your broiler, then broil the cake very briefly, until the meringue is golden. Cut into slices and serve. (Leftovers will keep in an airtight container in the fridge for up to 3 days.)

SUMMERY ETON MESS

An exciting twist on a British summertime favorite. You can use plain kisses or mix and match flavors like blueberry and raspberry (see page 32) to create a delicious seasonal Eton mess. Well, actually, it's not that messy . . . rather beautiful, we think.

SERVES 6 TO 8

1 batch Meringue Girls
  Mixture (page 26)

FOR THE RASPBERRY COULIS:

1½ cups/250 g frozen raspberries

1 tbsp honey, plus more
  if needed

4 cups/680 g fresh raspberries,
  blueberries, or strawberries

2 cups heavy cream

2 tbsp confectioners' sugar

2 tbsp freeze-dried raspberries
  (optional)

Make your meringue kisses following the instructions on pages 34 to 35.

To make the raspberry coulis: Put the frozen raspberries in a small saucepan, drizzle in the honey, and set the pan over medium heat. Once the berries are simmering, turn down the heat to maintain a gentle bubbling and cook until lightly thickened, about 10 minutes. Remove from the heat and let cool slightly. Taste the mixture and stir in more honey if it needs it, but you want the coulis to be quite tart as the meringues are very sweet. Using an immersion blender, purée until smooth, and then let cool completely.

If you are using strawberries, hull and quarter them. In a large bowl, whip the cream and sugar to soft peaks, taking care not to overwhip.

When you are ready to serve—and only then—start assembling the dessert. If you do this too early, you'll end up with a soggy mess, not Eton mess. Divide the meringue kisses among individual bowls. Dollop whipped cream around the meringues and top with the fresh berries. Spoon coulis over everything and crumble the freeze-dried raspberries (if using) over the centers. Serve right away.

POMEGRANATE MERINGUE SLAB

Ruby red pomegranate seeds, crème fraîche, chopped pistachio, and a quick-and-easy mint sugar on top of baked meringue. This Middle Eastern–inspired sweet looks and tastes the business.

SERVES 8

1 batch Meringue Girls
  Mixture (page 26)
½ tsp natural pink food coloring
Leaves from 1 small bunch
  fresh mint
¼ cup/50 g superfine sugar
1 cup/600 g crème fraîche
1 cup/100 g fresh pomegranate
  seeds
¾ cup/100 g chopped roasted
  pistachios
2 tbsp pomegranate molasses

Preheat the oven to 200°F.

Dab a blob of meringue on each corner of a baking sheet, then line the sheet with parchment paper, using the meringue blobs to glue it down.

Scrape the meringue onto the corner of the prepared baking sheet and use the back of a large spoon to spread it into a rough 8½-by-11-inch rectangle. With the tip of a knife, swirl in the food coloring to create a marbled effect.

Bake for 1 hour, or until the meringue is crisp on the outside and easily lifts off the parchment paper with its base intact. Let cool completely on the baking sheet.

In a food processor, blend the mint and sugar until the mixture is dark green and well combined, or crush them together using a mortar and pestle.

When you're ready to serve, dollop the crème fraîche onto the meringue, sprinkle on the pomegranate seeds and pistachios, then spoon on the mint sugar. To finish, drizzle with the pomegranate molasses. Cut into pieces and serve.

LEMON SORBET MERINGUE CRUNCH

This lovely summer party treat is another tasty way of using up broken or dried-out meringues. The sweet, crushed meringue balances out the tangy lemon sorbet and gives a brilliant texture—a match made in heaven. If you don't want to make your own sorbet, using store-bought is fine.

SERVES 4 TO 6

FOR THE LEMON SORBET:
1¾ cups plus 2 tbsp/500 g
   superfine sugar
2⅓ cups water
¾ cup fresh lemon juice
   (from 5 or 6 lemons)
Grated zest of 1 small lemon

½ batch Meringue Girls Mixture
   (page 26), flavored to suit your
   taste and formed into 18 kisses
   (see pages 30 to 35), then dried
   out for up to 2 weeks
4 to 6 sugar cones

To make the sorbet: Pour the sugar and water into a medium heavy-bottomed saucepan. Heat gently over medium heat, stirring occasionally until the sugar dissolves, then simmer for a couple of minutes. Transfer to a container, stir in the lemon juice and zest, and let cool. Cover and refrigerate until well chilled.

Churn the chilled liquid in an ice cream machine, then freeze the sorbet until it is firm and scoopable. Alternatively, pour it into a shallow container, place in the freezer, and beat the mixture with a fork every 30 minutes until it has a smooth sorbet-like texture.

Crush about 10 of the meringues into fine crumbs (reserve the rest for another use) and scatter onto a flat tray. Scoop balls of sorbet, rolling each one in meringue crumbs until completely covered, then set the scoop on a cone and serve right away.

PISTACHIO AND ROSE WATER PAVLOVA WITH GREEK YOGURT, HONEY, AND FIGS

This Middle Eastern–inspired Pavlova uses Greek yogurt instead of cream. Topped with figs, pistachios, honey, and fresh rose petals, it's a stunning dessert.

SERVES 6 TO 8

1 batch Meringue Girls Mixture (page 26)
¾ cup/100 g pistachios, shelled
1 tbsp rose water
6 fresh figs
1¼ cups/300 g Greek yogurt
¼ cup honey
8 to 10 fresh red or pink rose petals

Preheat your oven to 200°F.

Dab a blob of meringue on each corner of a baking sheet, then line the sheet with parchment paper, using the meringue like glue to stick the paper down.

Finely grind half of the pistachios. Gently fold one-half of the ground pistachios along with the rose water into the meringue mixture. Be very careful not to knock out any of the volume.

Working quickly, spoon the meringue mixture onto the center of the prepared baking sheet and shape into a 10-inch spiky circle with your spoon. Then use the back of the spoon to form a large well in the center of the meringue. Sprinkle with the rest of the ground pistachios and bake for about 2 hours, or until the meringue is crisp on the outside and easily lifts off the parchment. Let cool completely on the baking sheet.

Slice the figs into quarters and roughly chop the remaining pistachios. Now you are ready to plate up.

Remove the cooled meringue from the parchment and set it in the center of a serving platter. Spoon the yogurt into the well of the meringue, allowing some to ooze down the sides. Place most of the figs on top of the yogurt and scatter a few around the platter. Drizzle everything with the honey. Finish the masterpiece by scattering the chopped pistachios and fresh rose petals over the top.

MERINGUE RAINBOW CAKE

The mother of all rainbow cakes, this epic, bright layered meringue dessert takes a bit of work but is worth it.

SERVES 12

2 separate batches Meringue
  Girls Mixture (page 26)
Pink, red, orange, yellow, green,
  blue, and purple gel food
  coloring
2 cups heavy cream

Position three racks in the oven—in the bottom, middle, and upper parts—and preheat the oven to 200°F. Line three baking sheets with parchment paper and draw a 10-inch circle on each parchment sheet, using a plate or cake pan as a guide. Flip the parchment over so the outline is on the underside, but still visible, and glue down the corners of the parchment with dabs of meringue.

Divide your first batch of meringue mixture evenly among three clean bowls. Gently fold in a few drops of pink food coloring into the meringue in one bowl, followed by a few drops of red food coloring to make a bright red mixture. Fold a few drops of orange coloring into the meringue in another bowl and a few drops of yellow coloring into the last one.

Using the traced circles as guides, spread each of the colored meringue mixtures into a flat 10-inch disk of even thickness on the prepared baking sheets. Bake for 1 hour, or until the disks are easily lifted off the parchment paper. Let cool completely on the baking sheets.

Remove the first meringue disks from the baking sheets. Re-line the sheets with parchment paper, once again drawing circles and gluing down the parchment corners. Divide your second batch of meringue mixture evenly among three clean bowls and color one bowlful with a few drops of green coloring, one with blue, and one with purple. Form the colored meringues into disks, bake, and let cool as you did the first batch. (The baked and cooled disks can be kept in an airtight container in a cool, dry spot for up to 1 week.)

When you're ready to serve, use a stand mixer to whip the cream just until it holds firm peaks. Set the purple disk on a cake stand and spread about ¾ cup whipped cream over the surface, all the way to the edge. Continue to build your cake, layering the blue, green, yellow, orange, and red meringue disks—in that order—and the whipped cream. Serve right away.

NOTES: *We suggest making the meringue mixture in two batches, one at a time, and forming only six meringue layers (instead of seven, as shown in the photos on pages 76 and 77), because home ovens can't fit more than three baking sheets at a time. Use the first batch of meringue to make the red, orange, and yellow disks, and the second batch to make the green, blue, and purple ones.*

This is one of the few times we advocate using non-natural food dyes (Wilton gels work really well), in order to achieve vibrant colors that really pop. The trick to a bright red disk is to fold some pink dye through the meringue in order to get a nice base color, then fold in some red dye to enrich the hue.

If you like, you can flavor the meringue with vanilla. Split open two vanilla bean pods, scrape out the seeds, and fold a portion of the seeds into each bowlful of meringue after folding in the food coloring.

GRILLED PEACHES WITH CRUSHED AMARETTI COOKIES AND MAPLE MERINGUE

Our maple meringue has a lovely golden color and is absolutely delicious. Here, we use it dolloped on top of grilled peaches filled with crunchy amaretti cookies. For a super-summery dessert, try cooking the peaches on an outdoor grill.

SERVES 4

4 peaches, halved and pitted
8 to 12 amaretti cookies, crushed
Maple Meringue (page 153)
Maple syrup for drizzling

Preheat your oven to 350°F.

Heat a large ovenproof grill pan over medium-high heat until hot. Place the peach halves cut-side down in the pan and cook without moving them until dark grill lines have formed, about 4 minutes. Turn the peach halves over, slide the pan into the oven, and cook until the peaches are just softened (but not falling apart), about 10 minutes. If you'll be browning the meringue under the broiler, preheat the broiler.

Fill the center of each peach half with crushed amaretti cookies and dollop maple meringue on top. Brown the meringue under the broiler or with a kitchen torch until golden.

Carefully transfer the peaches to a serving platter or individual plates. Drizzle with maple syrup and serve right away.

wintery puddings

CHOCOLATE CHIP COOKIE MERINGUE SQUARES

A chewy chocolate chip cookie base, topped with baked brown-sugar meringue. So addictive.

MAKES 12 SQUARES

FOR THE COOKIE BASE:
¾ cup/170 g unsalted butter, melted, plus more for greasing
2 cups/250 g all-purpose flour
½ tsp baking soda
½ tsp salt
1 cup/200 g dark brown sugar
½ cup/100 g superfine sugar
1 tbsp vanilla extract
1 egg plus 1 egg yolk
2 cups/325 g chocolate chips

2 cups plus 3 tbsp/240 g dark brown sugar
120 g egg whites (from about 4 eggs)

To make the cookie base: Preheat the oven to 350°F. Butter a 9-by-13-in baking sheet and line with parchment paper cut to fit into the bottom and up the long sides of the pan, with some overhang. Grease the parchment with butter.

In a medium bowl, sift the flour, baking soda, and salt. In a large bowl, beat together the melted butter, brown sugar, and superfine sugar with a wooden spoon until well blended. Beat in the vanilla, egg, and egg yolk until light and creamy, then mix in the dry ingredients until just blended and a crumbly dough forms.

Gently press the dough into the bottom of the prepared baking sheet, making sure the surface is even. Sprinkle the chocolate chips over the cookie dough and press them down lightly. Bake for 15 minutes, until the dough is just cooked but still soft. Let cool on a wire rack.

Turn up the oven temperature to 400°F. Using the brown sugar and egg whites, make the meringue, following the instructions on page 26.

Using a rubber spatula, mound the meringue onto the center of the cookie base and spread it to the edges. Cut a sheet of parchment paper about the same size as the pan and lightly press it onto the meringue. Turn down the oven temperature to 350°F and bake the meringue-topped cookie for 10 minutes, then remove the parchment and bake for about 5 minutes longer, or until the meringue peaks are lightly golden.

Let cool completely on a wire rack, then cut into 12 squares.

HONEYCOMB, CHOCOLATE, AND SALTED PEANUT MERINGUES

Big, spiky, and chewy meringues rolled in honeycomb candy, cocoa, and salted peanuts. These sweet and slightly salty meringues are delicious eaten just as they are. To take them over the edge, drizzle with melted milk chocolate and serve with a big dollop of Greek yogurt.

MAKES 6 BIG ONES

1 Crunchie bar or a small block of honeycomb candy, crumbled

½ cup/40 g good-quality cocoa powder

1 batch Meringue Girls Mixture (page 26)

½ cup/50 g roasted salted peanuts, roughly chopped

Line a baking sheet with parchment paper. Preheat the oven to 200°F.

Carefully fold one-half of the crumbled Crunchie bar and 1 tbsp of the cocoa powder into the meringue mixture.

Scatter the remaining crumbled Crunchie bar, the remaining 7 tbsp cocoa powder, and the chopped peanuts in a pie plate or shallow baking dish.

Using two large metal spoons, scoop up about one-sixth of the meringue, roll the mound in the candy-cocoa-peanut mixture until nicely coated, and set it on the prepared baking sheet. Repeat with the remaining meringue and coating, spacing the mounds evenly apart.

Bake for 2 hours, or until the meringues easily lift off the parchment paper with their bases intact. Let cool on the baking sheet or a wire rack.

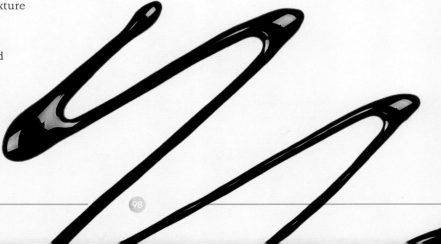

FROZEN BERRIES AND HOT CUSTARD WITH MERINGUE KISSES

Such a simple but delicious combination using frozen berries, custard sauce, and meringue kisses. The hot custard thaws the berries and melts the meringues ever so slightly. Hot, cold, fresh, and crunchy—a delight for the palate.

SERVES 8

½ batch Meringue Girls Mixture
(page 26)
4 cups/680 g frozen mixed
berries
Vanilla Custard
(page 143), warm

Make your meringue kisses following the instructions on pages 34 to 35.

Divide the frozen berries among eight individual serving bowls and top with a meringue kiss or two. Bring the bowls to the table, along with the warm custard in a pitcher, and allow each of your guests to pour custard over his or her bowlful. Eat right away.

PRETZEL AND CHOCOLATE
MARSHMALLOW MERINGUE TART

A no-bake, sweet-salty crust, topped with rich chocolate and chewy marshmallow meringue. Everyone asks us for this recipe.

SERVES 6 TO 8

FOR THE CRUST:

7 tbsp/100 g butter, plus more
  for greasing
3½ oz/100 g salted pretzels
3½ oz/100 g plain digestive
  biscuits such as McVitie's
¼ cup/55 g Lyle's Golden Syrup

FOR THE FILLING:

14 oz 70% dark
  chocolate, chopped
2 cups heavy cream at room
  temperature
A large pinch of Maldon sea salt

Marshmallow Meringue
  (page 148)
A couple handfuls of salted
  pretzels

To make the crust: Brush an 8-inch removable-bottomed tart pan with a little butter.

In a food processor, grind the pretzels and digestive biscuits to fine crumbs, or place in a plastic bag and bash with a rolling pin. Pour the crumbs into a medium bowl.

In a small saucepan, heat the butter and golden syrup over medium heat, stirring, until the butter has melted. Drizzle onto the crumbs and mix until evenly moistened. Empty the mixture into your prepared tart pan and, using the back of a spoon, firmly press it into an even layer in the bottom of the pan. Refrigerate the crust until set, about 2 hours.

To make the filling: Melt the chocolate in a heatproof bowl set over a saucepan of simmering water, or put it into a microwave-safe bowl and heat it at high power for 1 to 2 minutes until melted. Add the cream and salt and stir until the mixture is thick and smooth. Pour the filling into the crust and refrigerate until set, about 2 hours, or up to 2 days.

Spread the Marshmallow Meringue over the filling and refrigerate until set, about 30 minutes. Scatter the pretzels across the surface and remove the tart from the pan. Cut into slices with a knife dipped in hot water and serve.

PASSION FRUIT
MERINGUE FILO TARTLETS

Everyone goes crazy for these mini tarts. Filo pastry is sold frozen. Let it fully defrost before separating the paper-thin sheets.

MAKES 12 TARTLETS

7 tbsp/100 g unsalted butter, melted, plus more for greasing
12 full-size filo pastry sheets, stacked
1 cup plus 2 tbsp/300 g Passion Fruit Curd (page 139)
Italian Meringue (page 150)
Pulp and seeds scooped from 2 fresh passion fruits

Preheat the oven to 350°F. Grease a 12-cup muffin pan with a little butter.

Cut the filo stack into quarters to make 48 rectangles. Take one quarter stack and cover the rest with plastic wrap to prevent the pastry from drying out. Brush the top rectangle with melted butter, then fit it into a muffin cup. Build up four filo layers in the cup, brushing each rectangle with butter and rotating it slightly so that the corners don't align in the cup. Line the remaining cups in the same way.

Bake the pastry for 7 minutes, or until lightly golden. Remove the pan from the oven and spoon in the curd, dividing it evenly among the shells and filling each one about three-fourths full.

Return the pan to the oven and bake for another 5 minutes, or until the curd is set and the edges of the shells are golden brown. Let cool on a wire rack. Leave the oven on if you will be using it to brown the meringue.

Pipe or dollop Italian meringue on top of each tartlet, completely covering the curd.

Brown the meringue with a kitchen torch or in the oven until golden. Spoon the fresh passion fruit pulp and seeds over the tartlets, carefully remove them from the pan, and serve.

SALTED CARAMEL, POACHED PEAR, AND CHOCOLATE DRIZZLE MERINGUE SLAB

Oozy caramel, poached pears, dark chocolate, mascarpone, and walnuts—this is an autumnal dessert dream. It's a perfect finale to a casual dinner party where everyone can just dig in.

SERVES 8

FOR THE MERINGUE BASE:

1 batch Meringue Girls
    Mixture (page 26)
2 tbsp good-quality cocoa
    powder, sifted

FOR THE POACHED PEARS:

4½ cups water
5 tbsp/65 g granulated sugar
1 cinnamon stick
4 firm but ripe pears

A large pinch of Maldon sea salt
½ cup caramel sauce
1 cup/225 g mascarpone cheese
3½ oz 70% dark chocolate,
    melted
1 cup/100 g walnut halves,
    toasted

To make the meringue base: Preheat your oven to 200°F. Dab a blob of meringue on each corner of a baking sheet, then line with parchment paper, using the meringue blobs to glue it down.

Gently fold the cocoa powder into the meringue mixture, taking care not to lose any volume. Scrape the meringue onto the center of the prepared baking sheet and use the back of a large spoon to spread it into a rough 8½-by-11-inch rectangle.

Bake for 1 hour, or until the meringue is crisp on the outside and easily lifts off the parchment with its base intact. Let cool completely on the baking sheet. Don't worry if the meringue cracks—you'll be smothering it with deliciousness, so cracks won't matter. (The meringue will keep in an airtight container, stored in a cool, dry place, for up to 2 weeks.)

To make the poached pears: In a medium, heavy-bottomed saucepan, bring the water to a boil over medium-high heat. Add the sugar and cinnamon stick and return to a boil, stirring to dissolve the sugar.

While the liquid is heating, peel the pears, cut them lengthwise into quarters, and remove the cores; leave the stems on for visual effect, if you like. Carefully add the pears to the boiling liquid, turn down the heat to low, and poach gently for 15 minutes, or until the tip of a paring knife easily slides into the center. Using a slotted spoon, remove the pears to a large plate.

When you're ready to serve, stir the salt into the caramel sauce. Set the meringue base on a serving platter or tray and dollop with the mascarpone. With your creative juices flowing, layer on the pears, pour on the caramel, drizzle with the chocolate, and sprinkle with the walnuts. Cut your masterpiece into pieces and serve.

MERINGUE LAYER CAKE
WITH CHOCOLATE AND BLACKBERRIES

This is a delicious and indulgent dinner party centerpiece.

SERVES 12

FOR THE MERINGUE LAYERS:
Double batch of Meringue Girls Mixture (page 26)
4 tsp cocoa, sifted

FOR THE COULIS:
2 cups/340 g blackberries (fresh or frozen)
1 tbsp honey

FOR THE GANACHE:
7 oz 70% dark chocolate, chopped
1¼ cups heavy cream, room temperature

FOR THE WHIPPED CREAM:
2½ cups heavy cream
1 tbsp confectioners' sugar
1 tbsp crème de cassis or Chambord liqueur (optional)

Cocoa powder for dusting
1 tbsp cacao nibs, crushed
1 cup/170 g fresh blackberries

Position racks in the upper and lower third of the oven and preheat your oven to 200°F. Line two baking sheets with parchment paper and draw two 8-inch circles on each parchment sheet, using a plate or cake pan as a guide. Flip the parchment over so the outlines are on the underside, but still visible, and glue down the corners of the parchment with dabs of meringue.

To make the meringue layers: Evenly divide the meringue mixture among the traced circles on the prepared baking sheets. Using an icing spatula and the circles as guides, spread the meringue into flat 8-inch disks of even thickness. Bake for 1 hour, or until the disks are easily lifted off the parchment paper. Let cool completely on the baking sheets, then dust each disk with 1 tsp of the cocoa powder.

To make the coulis: In a medium saucepan, combine the blackberries, honey, and 1 tbsp water. Bring to a boil over medium-high heat, then turn down the heat to maintain a gentle simmer and cook for 5 minutes, or until the berries have softened. Purée in a food processor until smooth. Set aside to cool.

To make the ganache: Melt the chocolate in a heatproof bowl set over a saucepan of simmering water, or put it into a microwave-safe bowl and heat it at high power for 1 to 2 minutes until melted. Add the cream, and stir until the mixture is thick and smooth.

To make the whipped cream: In a large bowl, whip the cream, confectioners' sugar, and crème de cassis (if using) just until the mixture holds its shape.

Place a meringue disk on a cake stand or platter. Using an icing spatula, spread one-third of the ganache on the meringue, all the way to the edges. Spread with one-third of the whipped cream, drizzle with one-third of the coulis, and then use a dinner knife to swirl the coulis into the cream to create a marbled effect. Repeat the layering using two more meringue disks and topping each with one-half of the remaining ganache, whipped cream, and coulis. Place the last meringue disk on top, dust with cocoa powder, and sprinkle on the cacao nibs. Scatter fresh blackberries on top and around the cake and serve.

BOOZY WINTER ETON MESS

A deliciously boozy concoction of Cointreau-soaked clementines and brandy cream, mixed with chocolate meringue kisses and decorated with pomegranate seeds. This makes a fantastic holiday dessert.

SERVES 8

FOR THE CLEMENTINES:
2½ cups Cointreau
4 clementines, peeled
   and segmented

1 batch Meringue Girls Mixture
   (page 26), flavored with
   chocolate (see page 30)

FOR THE BRANDY CREAM:
2½ cups heavy cream
¼ cup/25 g confectioners' sugar
A big splash of brandy

½ cup/50 g pomegranate, seeds
½ cup/30 g freeze-dried
   raspberries, crumbled (optional)

To prepare the clementines: Pour the Cointreau into a bowl and add the clementine segments. Stir, making sure all the segments get coated with the alcohol, then cover and leave to soak in the fridge for at least 2 hours, or ideally overnight.

Make your meringue kisses following the instructions on pages 34 to 35.

To make the brandy cream: In a large bowl, whip the cream and confectioners' sugar just until the mixture thickens. Be very careful not to overwhisk. Fold in the brandy with a spoon.

When you are ready to serve—and only then—start assembling the dessert. If you do this too early, you'll end up with a soggy mess. Spoon about ⅓ cup of brandy cream into each of eight individual serving bowls. Pile four meringue kisses into each bowl, then drizzle the remaining brandy cream over the meringues, dividing it evenly. Top with clementine segments and garnish with the pomegranate seeds and crumbled freeze-dried raspberries (if using). Serve right away.

GIANT MERINGUES

Giant meringues nearly as big as your head! We hope that Ottolenghi, the godfather of meringues, would be proud of these displayed in his window.

MAKES 6 BIG ONES

½ cup/50 g good-quality cocoa powder, sifted

¼ cup plus 2 tbsp/50 g cacao nibs (optional)

¾ cup/100 g shelled pistachios, finely chopped

1 batch of Meringue Girls Mixture (page 26)

Position racks in the upper and lower third of the oven and preheat your oven to 200°F. Line two baking sheets with parchment paper.

Scatter the cocoa powder and cacao nibs (if using) in a pie plate or shallow baking dish. Scatter the chopped pistachios in a second pie plate or baking dish.

Using two large metal spoons, scoop up about one-sixth of the meringue mixture, roll the mound in the cocoa until nicely coated, and set it on one of the prepared baking sheets. Form two more cocoa-coated mounds in the same way, evenly spacing them apart on the baking sheet.

Now form three pistachio-coated mounds with the remaining meringue mixture and the chopped pistachios, placing the meringues on the second baking sheet.

Bake the meringues for 3 hours, or until they easily lift off the parchment paper with their bases intact.

To serve, pile the meringues in a big, impressive stack.

MAPLE MERINGUE DOUGHNUTS WITH CARAMELIZED BANANAS

Gosh, these are good. Homemade doughnuts. Maple meringue. Caramelized bananas. Yum.

MAKES 6

FOR THE DOUGHNUTS:

Heaping 1 cup/160 g bread flour, plus more for dusting

¼ cup/50 g superfine sugar

2 tsp instant yeast

½ tsp salt

¼ cup whole milk, warmed

3 tbsp warm water

1½ tbsp unsalted butter, melted, plus more for greasing

1 egg, beaten

2 tsp ground cinnamon

2 qt vegetable oil

Maple Meringue (page 153)

2 bananas, peeled and sliced lengthwise into thirds

A splash of maple syrup

To make the doughnuts: In the bowl of your stand mixer, whisk together the flour, 1 tbsp of the sugar, the yeast, and the salt. In a small bowl, combine the warm milk and water, then add the butter and stir until the butter melts. Pour the liquid ingredients into the dry ingredients and add the beaten egg. Knead with the dough hook on low speed until a smooth, stretchy dough forms, about 10 minutes.

Lightly grease a large bowl with butter and place the dough in the bowl. Cover with a damp kitchen towel and let rise in a warm spot until the dough doubles in bulk, about 1 hour.

Transfer the dough to a lightly floured work surface and divide it into six evenly sized portions. Shape each piece into a ball and set on a lightly floured baking sheet, spacing them well apart. Cover with the damp kitchen towel and let rise again until doubled in bulk, about 45 minutes.

About 30 minutes into the second rise, in a small bowl, stir together the cinnamon and remaining 3 tbsp sugar. Attach a deep-fry thermometer to a large, deep, heavy-bottomed saucepan and pour in the oil. Heat over high heat until the oil registers 325°F on the thermometer. When the dough balls are ready, working in two batches, fry the doughnuts for about 3 minutes per side, until golden brown. Transfer them to a paper towel–lined plate and sprinkle with cinnamon sugar until nicely coated all around. Let cool slightly.

Fit a piping bag with a ½-inch plain tip and put the meringue into the bag. Using the tip of a sharp knife, poke

a small hole in the side of each doughnut, insert the piping tip into the hole, and fill the center with as much meringue as it will hold.

Heat a large skillet over medium-high heat. Add the banana slices and maple syrup and cook until the bananas are deep golden brown, about 6 minutes. Lay one banana slice over each doughnut and serve right away.

SPICED APPLES WITH SALTED CRUMBLE, CINNAMON KISSES, AND VANILLA CUSTARD

This pudding is our take on the classic apple crumble, with cinnamon meringue kisses and a salty crumble topping.

SERVES 4

1 batch Meringue Girls Mixture (page 26), flavored with cinnamon (see page 31)

FOR THE CRUMBLE:
¼ cup plus 2 tbsp/50 g all-purpose flour
¼ cup/50 g superfine sugar
1 tsp flaky sea salt
3½ tbsp unsalted butter, at room temperature
¼ cup/50 g sliced almonds

FOR THE APPLES:
4 Granny Smith apples, quartered and cored
1 tbsp water
1 tbsp dark brown sugar
2 cinnamon sticks

FOR SERVING:
Vanilla Custard (page 143), warm

Make your meringue kisses following the instructions on pages 34 to 35.

Preheat the oven to 350°F.

To make the crumble: In a medium bowl, whisk together the flour, superfine sugar, and salt. Add the butter and mix with your fingertips until the mixture resembles bread crumbs. Stir in the almonds.

Scatter the crumble mixture on a baking sheet and bake for about 15 minutes, tossing occasionally, until golden brown. Let cool on the baking sheet.

To prepare the apples: In a large saucepan, combine the apple quarters, water, brown sugar, and cinnamon sticks. Bring to a simmer over medium-high heat, stirring occasionally, then turn down the heat to maintain a gentle simmer. Cover and cook until the apples are tender but not mushy, about 20 minutes.

To serve: Divide the warm apples among four individual bowls. Top each with 3 or 4 cinnamon kisses (reserve the rest for another use), then pour over some warm custard. Sprinkle with a portion of the crumble and serve right away.

Gift IDEAS

CHEWY PISTACHIO COFFEE DUNKERS

The ultimate coffee dunkers, these cookies have a crisp outside and chewy middle, with a delicate green color on the inside and a deep pistachio taste. Cut any shape you like—we use our *M* and *G* cookie cutters—and dunk them into your favorite mug.

MAKES 12 COOKIES

Butter for greasing
1 tsp vanilla extract
1 tsp white wine vinegar
1 batch Meringue Girls Mixture
  (page 26)
3 cups/350 g shelled pistachios,
  finely ground

Preheat the oven to 375°F. Grease a 9-by-13-inch rimmed baking sheet with butter, line it with parchment paper, and grease the parchment.

Carefully fold the vanilla extract and vinegar (vinegar is what gives baked meringue a lovely chewy middle) into the meringue mixture, and then fold in the ground pistachios.

Spoon the mixture into the prepared baking sheet, carefully spread it to the edges, and smooth the surface; it should be about ¾ inch thick. Bake for 30 to 40 minutes, until golden; the middle will still be a bit gooey, but it will harden as it cools. Let cool completely in the baking sheet.

Cut the meringue into 12 squares or use cookie cutters to stamp out shapes. Carefully remove the cookies from the parchment paper. These make a lovely gift and keep well for up to 1 week in an airtight container.

MERINGUE EASTER EGGS

These egg-shaped treats are made by sandwiching two baked meringues around a chocolate filling; a dusting of cocoa adds a whimsical speckled appearance. This is a fun activity to do with children, and the eggs are perfect for giving as Easter gifts. To present them, you can put them into an egg carton, tie the package with ribbon, and tuck a feather into the bow. Or use straw to create little nests for the eggs to sit in and set the nested eggs in a box.

MAKES ABOUT 12 EGGS

A few drops of natural food
  coloring in the color of
  your choice
½ batch Meringue Girls Mixture
  (page 26)
Cocoa powder for dusting
Chocolate Ganache (page 38)

Preheat the oven to 200°F. Dab a blob of meringue on each corner of a baking sheet then line with parchment paper, using the blobs to glue it down.

Fold the food coloring into the meringue mixture to make a light pastel shade. Put the meringue into a large piping bag with a 1-inch opening, or use a disposable piping bag and cut the tip to a 1-inch opening after filling. Pipe about twenty-four 2-inch mounds of meringue (see page 35 for help with piping) onto the prepared baking sheet, spacing them about ¾ inch apart. Moisten your fingertip with water and carefully smooth out the tips and round the surfaces of the meringue mounds, creating a dome shape. Dust each one with a tiny pinch of cocoa powder.

Bake for 30 to 40 minutes, or until the meringues come off the parchment paper easily with their bases intact. Let cool completely on the baking sheet.

Using a small spatula or knife, spread the bottom of each meringue with about 2 tsp of the chocolate ganache. Form the eggs by putting two meringues together, chocolate side to chocolate side. These make a lovely gift and keep well for up to 1 week in an airtight container.

MERINGUE ALPHABET

Why stick to piping only kisses? Get creative with the alphabet. Bake the letters of a friend's name, or a message like "happy birthday." Meringue letters are great for kids' parties or big romantic gestures. Or you could make the letters small to decorate the top of a cake. As you pipe, remember that the meringue will expand a bit in the oven. We use non-natural gel food colorings here to achieve stronger, more vibrant hues. You'll need a piping bag for each color; disposable bags are an easy and inexpensive option.

MAKES ABOUT
FIFTEEN 4-INCH
LETTERS

1 batch Meringue Girls
   Mixture (page 26)
Gel food coloring in the
   colors of your choice

Position three racks in the oven—in the bottom, middle, and upper part—and preheat your oven to 200°F. Line three baking sheets with parchment paper and glue down the corners of the parchment with dabs of meringue.

For each food coloring that you use, brush the inside bottom 2 inches of a disposable piping bag (the area near the tip) with coloring. Fill the bag with meringue mixture and twist the open end of the bag to push the meringue down to the bottom. Cut a ¾-inch opening at the tip of the bag and pipe your letters onto the prepared baking sheet, spacing them about 1 inch apart.

When all your letters have been piped, bake for 1 hour, or until firm and the meringues can be lifted off the parchment with ease. Be gentle, because the letters are fragile. Let cool completely on the baking sheets. These will keep for up to 1 week in an airtight container.

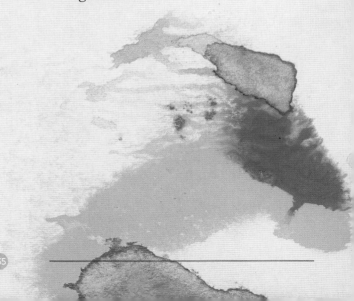

USING YOUR YOLKS

PASSION FRUIT CURD

Use this zingy passion fruit curd as the filling for the tartlets on page 107. If you can find fresh passion fruit, to get pulp, cut the fruits in half, scoop out the insides, and strain to remove the seeds. You'll need 10 to 12 fresh passion fruits for this recipe. Or you can use frozen passion fruit pulp, which is often sold in Latin American grocery stores or well-stocked supermarkets and specialty shops.

MAKES ABOUT 2 CUPS

⅔ cup passion fruit pulp
1 tbsp fresh lemon juice
¾ cup plus 2 tbsp/170 g chilled
   unsalted butter, cut into cubes
1 cup/200 g superfine sugar
5 egg yolks

Place the passion fruit pulp, lemon juice, butter, and sugar in a medium-size, heavy-bottomed saucepan. Set the pan over medium heat and stir until the butter has melted and the sugar has dissolved.

In a medium bowl, whisk the egg yolks until combined. While whisking continuously, gradually add the hot passion fruit mixture to the egg yolks, then pour the passion fruit–yolk mixture back into the pan. Cook over low heat, stirring, until the curd is thick enough to coat the back of a spoon, 6 to 7 minutes.

Transfer the curd to a bowl and let cool completely. If not using immediately, cover with plastic wrap or put in an airtight container and store in the fridge for up to 2 weeks.

LEMON CURD WITH LEMONGRASS

We LOVE tangy, creamy lemon curd. It's one of life's simple pleasures. You can buy lemon curd, but it's really satisfying to make your own. Our version includes lemongrass, and we sometimes add a fresh chile for a little heat. Make it on a rainy day and keep it in the fridge, or give some to friends as a home-made gift.

MAKES ABOUT 2 CUPS

1 stalk lemongrass, white part
  only, bruised with a knife
1 fresh red chile, sliced
  lengthwise (optional)
Grated zest and juice of 2 lemons
1 cup plus 2 tbsp/225 g superfine
  sugar
½ cup/60 g chilled unsalted
  butter, cut into cubes
2 eggs, plus 2 egg yolks
1 tsp cornstarch
1 tsp water

In a medium, heavy-bottomed saucepan, combine the lemongrass, chile (if using), lemon zest and juice, sugar, and butter. Cook over medium heat, stirring, until the butter has melted and the sugar has completely dissolved. Strain through a sieve set over a bowl.

In a medium bowl, lightly whisk together the eggs and egg yolks. While whisking continuously so that the eggs don't scramble, slowly pour in the hot lemon mixture. Once it has all been added, whisk until well combined. In a small bowl, stir together the cornstarch and water until smooth, then whisk this slurry into the egg-lemon mixture. Pour the egg-lemon mixture back into the saucepan and cook over low heat, stirring continuously, until the curd is thick enough to coat the back of a spoon, about 10 minutes.

Remove the pan from the heat and let the curd cool completely, stirring occasionally. Once cooled, transfer to a container, cover tightly, and refrigerate until ready to use, or for up to 1 week.

CHEATER'S LEMON CURD TART FILLING

This is the easiest way to make a delicious citrus curd tart filling. It's so simple and quick but works like a dream. We've stayed with the classic lemon curd here, but feel free to substitute lime or grapefruit juice for the lemon juice. The recipe makes enough to fill an 8-inch tart shell; prebake the shell, pour in the curd, and then bake at 325°F for 15 minutes, or until the filling has just set. Let the tart cool completely before serving.

MAKES ABOUT 2 CUPS

3 egg yolks

One 14-ounce can cold sweetened condensed milk

Grated zest and juice of 4 lemons (grapefruit, blood orange, or lime juice will work, too)

Chill all of your bowls and beaters for at least 30 minutes before beginning. In a medium bowl, beat the egg yolks with a handheld mixer for 2 minutes, or until thickened and pale in color. Add the condensed milk and beat until for 3 minutes, or until you see trails in the thickening mixture. Finally, add the lemon zest and juice and beat until well combined and peaks form, about 4 minutes. Transfer to a container, cover tightly, and refrigerate until ready to use, or for up to 1 week.

VANILLA CUSTARD

This classic vanilla custard sauce is a great way to use up spare egg yolks. If you like, you can use a vanilla bean instead of vanilla extract. Split the pod in half lengthwise and scrape out the seeds. Add both the pod and the seeds to milk mixture in the saucepan and bring to a simmer, then remove the pan from the heat, cover, and let the flavors infuse for a few minutes. Remove the pod halves, then continue with the recipe.

MAKES ABOUT 2½ CUPS

2⅓ cups whole milk
¼ cup half-and-half
4 egg yolks
2½ tbsp superfine sugar
2 tsp cornstarch
1 tbsp vanilla extract

In a small, heavy-bottomed saucepan, bring the milk and half-and-half to a simmer over low heat.

In a medium bowl, whisk together the egg yolks, sugar, and cornstarch. While whisking continuously, slowly pour in the hot milk mixture, then return the mixture to the saucepan. Bring to a simmer over low heat, stirring constantly with a wooden spoon. As you stir, scrape along the bottom of the pan, feeling for a silky, slippery texture that indicates that the custard is beginning to thicken.

As soon as the custard is thick enough to coat the back of the spoon, pour it through a sieve set over a bowl to remove any lumps.

Add the vanilla extract and serve immediately, or if you want to keep the custard hot for a while, pour it into a pitcher, cover with plastic wrap, and set the pitcher in a warm-water bath.

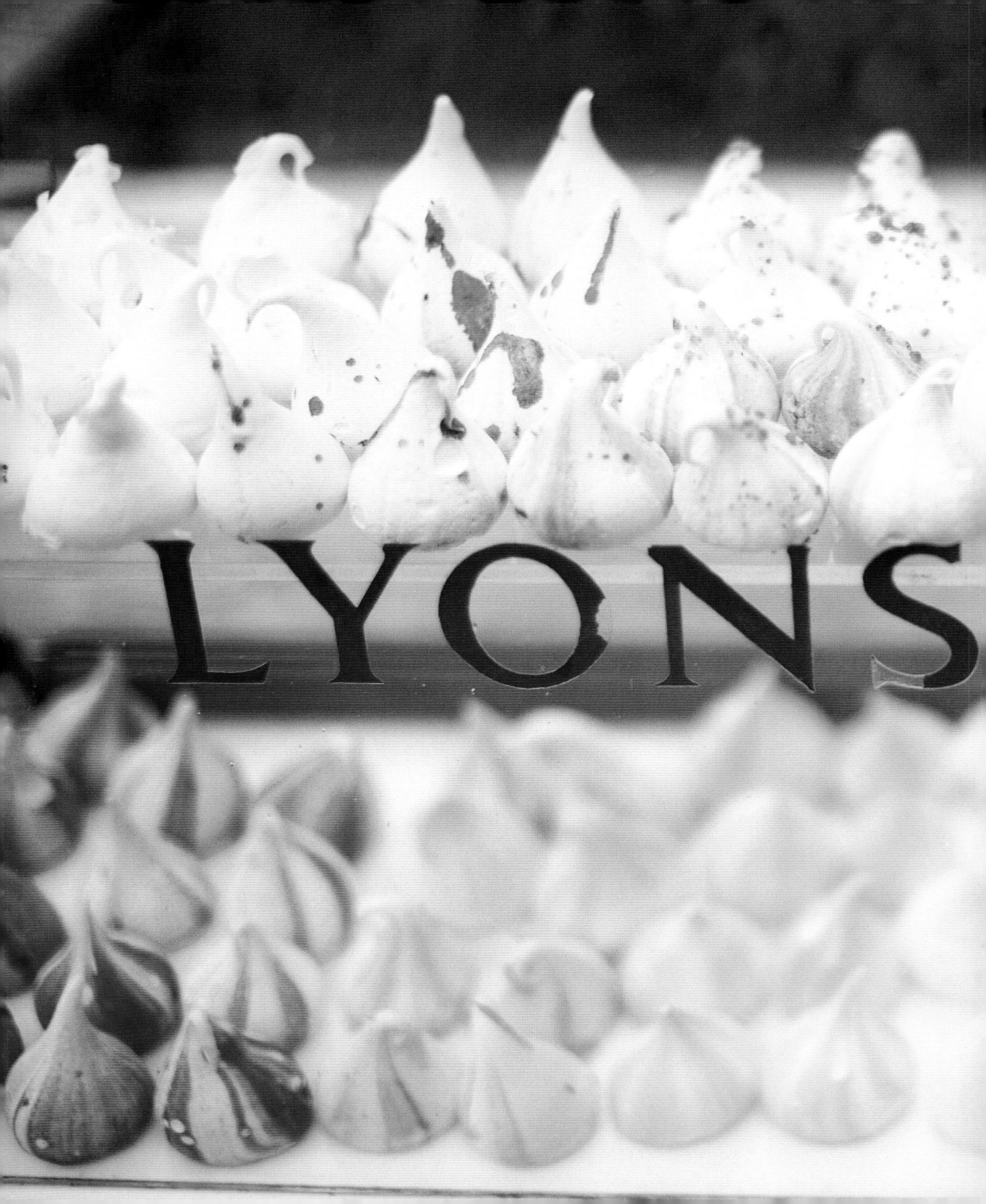
LYONS

CAKES

other MERINGUE methods

MARSHMALLOW MERINGUE

This recipe makes a really gooey meringue. When chilled, the marshmallows set the mixture so you get an extra thick and mallowy texture. This meringue is delicious on the no-bake pretzel and chocolate tart on page 105, or use it as a topping for any sweet tart or cake.

MAKES 2 CUPS

150 g superfine sugar (¾ cup)
75 g egg whites
  (from about 2½ eggs)
110 g marshmallow creme (½ cup)

Preheat the oven to 400°F.

Line a rimmed baking sheet with parchment paper, pour in the sugar, and put the baking sheet in the oven for about 5 minutes, until the edges of the sugar are just beginning to melt. Heating the sugar will help it dissolve in the egg whites more quickly and help create a glossy, stable mixture.

Meanwhile, make sure the bowl and whisk attachment of your standing mixer are free from grease. Pour the egg whites into the bowl. Whisk on low speed at first, allowing small bubbles to form, then increase the speed to high and continue whisking until the egg whites form stiff peaks and the bowl can be tipped upside down without the whites falling out. Stop whisking just before the whites take on a cotton-woolly appearance; if they do, they have been over-whisked and the egg white protein has lost some elasticity.

By now, the sugar should be ready to take out of the oven. With the whites stiff and while whisking again at high

148

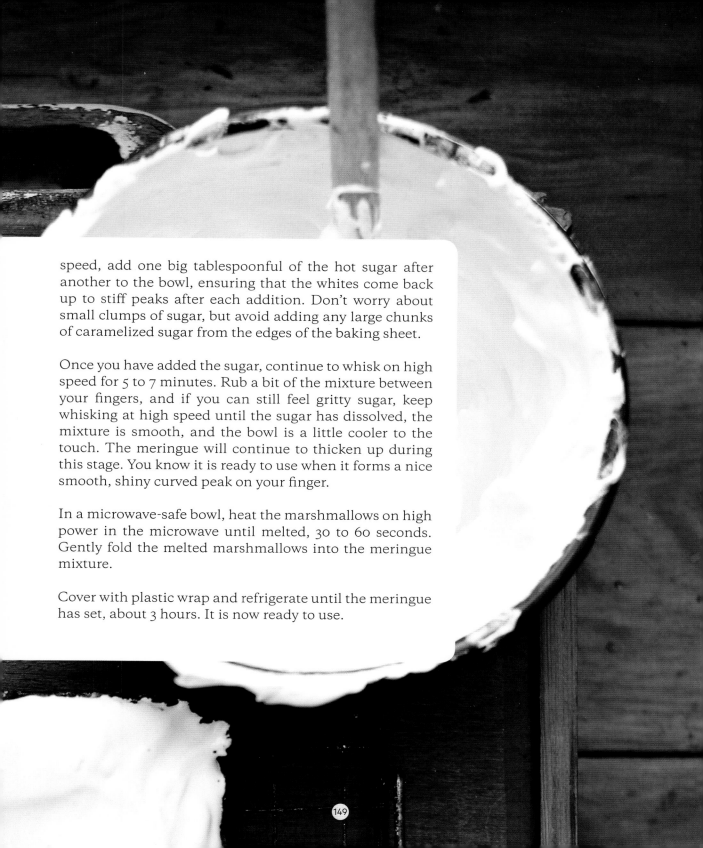

speed, add one big tablespoonful of the hot sugar after another to the bowl, ensuring that the whites come back up to stiff peaks after each addition. Don't worry about small clumps of sugar, but avoid adding any large chunks of caramelized sugar from the edges of the baking sheet.

Once you have added the sugar, continue to whisk on high speed for 5 to 7 minutes. Rub a bit of the mixture between your fingers, and if you can still feel gritty sugar, keep whisking at high speed until the sugar has dissolved, the mixture is smooth, and the bowl is a little cooler to the touch. The meringue will continue to thicken up during this stage. You know it is ready to use when it forms a nice smooth, shiny curved peak on your finger.

In a microwave-safe bowl, heat the marshmallows on high power in the microwave until melted, 30 to 60 seconds. Gently fold the melted marshmallows into the meringue mixture.

Cover with plastic wrap and refrigerate until the meringue has set, about 3 hours. It is now ready to use.

ITALIAN MERINGUE

The Italian meringue method involves making a sugar syrup, which is beaten while still hot into the stiff egg whites to cook the meringue on the spot. There is no need to bake Italian meringue, so it's a great mixture to use as a topping, as for the Lemon Meringue Tart (page 84) and Passion Fruit Meringue Filo Tarts (page 107).

MAKES 3 CUPS

115 g granulated sugar
(½ cup plus 1 tbsp)
3 tbsp water
60 g egg whites
(from about 2 eggs)

Pour the sugar and water into a small heavy-bottomed saucepan and attach a candy thermometer to the pan, if you have one. Slowly bring the mixture to a boil over medium-low heat, stirring occasionally with a wooden spoon. Have a pastry brush and a cup of cold water on hand to wash down any sugar crystals that get stuck to the side of the pan. If you let them build up, they will attract other bits of sugar and the sugar won't dissolve well.

The syrup is ready when it registers 250°F on the candy thermometer. If you are not using a thermometer, test the syrup by dropping a small teaspoonful into a cup of cold water; it should set into a firm ball that can be squashed between your fingers. If it just dissolves into the water, the syrup is not yet ready. If it sets into a hard ball, like a hard candy, the syrup is too hot for making Italian meringue; let it cool for 2 minutes or so to bring it down to the correct temperature.

While the syrup is cooking, whisk the egg whites on low speed in a stand mixer until frothy, then increase the speed to high and continue whisking until they form stiff peaks.

As soon as the syrup is ready, turn the mixer speed to medium and pour the hot syrup onto the whites in a slow, steady stream. Try not to pour it onto the wires of the whisk as it will quickly harden and stick to the cool metal.

Once you've added all the syrup, whisk on high speed until the mixture is stiff, shiny, and cooled, which will take 5 to 7 minutes. The meringue is now ready to use.

If you are using the meringue as a pie topping, after applying it, you can brown it with a kitchen torch or under a preheated broiler.

MAPLE MERINGUE

This maple meringue uses natural maple syrup instead of refined sugar. It's made like an Italian meringue—you heat the syrup to a high temperature and add it to the stiff egg whites. The earthy and rich maple flavor really comes through. The meringue doesn't need to be baked, so it's perfect for our Maple Meringue Doughnuts on page 119. It also works really well in recipes for baked meringues (you can make kisses with it) or as a topping for waffles. You will need a candy thermometer for cooking the syrup.

MAKES 3 CUPS

½ cup maple syrup
60 g egg whites
  (from about 2 eggs)

Put the maple syrup in a small heavy-bottomed saucepan and attach a candy thermometer to the pan. Place over medium heat.

When the syrup approaches 220°F, begin whisking the egg whites on low speed in a stand mixer. When they're frothy, increase the speed to high and beat until the whites hold stiff peaks.

When the syrup has come up to 235°F, turn the mixer speed to medium and slowly stream in the hot maple syrup. Once you've added all the syrup, whisk on high speed until the meringue is thick and a little shiny; this will take 5 to 7 minutes. The meringue is now ready to use.

Stacey Loves

LONG SKIRTS
Thrift Shop Bargains
3 SUGARS IN HER TEA
RED LIPSTICK
Japanese Anime
AND BJÖRK

Alex Loves

BOSTON TERRIERS
Gold Disco Pants
FOOD STYLING
VINTAGE KITCHENALIA
& Pomegranate Prosecco

SCAN WITH
layar

SEE PAGE 4
for instructions

INDEX

We would like to thank . . .

DAVID LOFTUS, undoubtably the world's best food photographer, for believing in the underdogs and for educating us on the rules of Instagram etiquette! Without you, this book would be nowhere nearly as beautiful as it is.

The team at SQUARE PEG, especially ROWAN YAPP for her belief in us and our occasional off-the-wall ideas!

DOUG KERR and GEMMA GERMAINS from our brilliant design team at WELL MADE STUDIO, who hit the nail on the head, and also KENN GOODALL for the painted titles.

Alex's parents, LAURIE HOFFLER & NICKY STEPHENSON aka MUMMA & PAPA LOUIGI. Thank you for everything, I love you both more than the universe.

Stacey's parents, SUE & BRENDAN O'GORMAN aka MAMA GORM & PAPA GORM, for their never-ending support from a far. Also, GRANDMA & GRANDPA BLAIR for their generosity and AUNTIE CAROL for her award-winning recipe development ideas.

TIM ETCHELLS for all his fantastic advice and for putting the MG wheels in motion.

SIAN O'GORMAN, for being the best sister in the world, for her creative genius and eye for design, and for being the creator of the Meringue Girls logo.

NEIL "REAL" BURNELL for all your love and support over eight wonderful years, and for keeping the bed warm for me after long nights of baking.

BRADY POLKIE for always keeping my spirits up. I am the luckiest girl in the world.

NICO RILLA, our incredibly supportive head chef (and second dad). Meringue Girls would not exist without you.

All the teachers at LEITHS SCHOOL OF FOOD AND WINE for their fantastic instruction, and all the LEITHS STUDENTS that have helped us along the way.

GIZZI ERSKINE for seeing something in us and always having our back.

JO HARRIS at TOPHAM STREET for her incredible eye for style and general loveliness.

CLAIRE STRICKETT (our first ever MG employee!) for not only being a pro meringue maker, but also for her general amazingness and help with all aspects of the business.

MELISSA BAKTH at SQUASH BANANA DESIGNS for her beautiful website, and her continued support.

ANDY FERNANDEZ for her exquiste hand modeling and help on the book shoot.

DEAN BRETT SCHNEIDER, the master baker, for giving us the time to pick your brain, and for all your mentoring advice.

MARTYN and the whole team at HAPPY KITCHEN for so generously sharing their space with us.

MATT YOUNG, aka VAN BLANC, who is the classiest white-van man in town.

DENIS from DENEEMOTION, for our wonderful videos.

BECCA GRAHAM, the best PR girl you could ever wish for, and the best chance meeting on Gumtree.

ASHLEE ACKLAND, for your incredible data entry skills and general awesomeness.

Meringue Girls x